T0208121

THE BABY TRAIL

Written by Callie Thompson

Illustrated by Jessica Wetterer

Copyright © 2022 Callie Thompson.

All rights reserved. No part of this book may be used or reproduced by any means, graphic, electronic, or mechanical, including photocopying, recording, taping or by any information storage retrieval system without the written permission of the author except in the case of brief quotations embodied in critical articles and reviews.

This is a work of fiction. All of the characters, names, incidents, organizations, and dialogue in this novel are either the products of the author's imagination or are used fictitiously.

Archway Publishing books may be ordered through booksellers or by contacting:

Archway Publishing
1663 Liberty Drive
Bloomington, IN 47403
www.archwaypublishing.com
844-669-3957

Because of the dynamic nature of the Internet, any web addresses or links contained in this book may have changed since publication and may no longer be valid. The views expressed in this work are solely those of the author and do not necessarily reflect the views of the publisher, and the publisher hereby disclaims any responsibility for them.

Any people depicted in stock imagery provided by Getty Images are models, and such images are being used for illustrative purposes only.
Certain stock imagery © Getty Images.

ISBN: 978-1-6657-2038-0 (sc)
ISBN: 978-1-6657-2037-3 (hc)
ISBN: 978-1-6657-2039-7 (e)

Print information available on the last page.

Archway Publishing rev. date: 9/30/2022

The Baby Trail

Hiked by Emily and John
For Mateo and Arlo. We love you 10x.

With gratitude to the inspiring parents of
Zoë, Jordan, Jane, George, August, Penny, Lake, and Sara.
(We can't tell which is which.)

Author Callie Thompson

Callie Thompson and her son Mateo enjoy creating adventure-filled bedtime stories and reading together each night ("three books because I'm three!"). Originally writing "The Baby Trail" as a poem for close friends after their IVF journey, Callie decided to turn it into a children's book after reconnecting with childhood friend and talented illustrator, Jessica Wetterer.

Jessica Wetterer is a published illustrator and designer. She has been drawing since she could hold a pencil. Animals have always been one of her favorite subjects! Some of the characters here were inspired by her sisters and friends as they've journeyed the Baby Trail. Her work can be found at JessicaWetterer.com

Illustrator Jessica Wetterer

Every day around the globe, parents start their quest.

Some go north, others south. Some go east or west.

They gather at the Baby Trail in the cold or heat—
ready to begin their search for babes they've yet to meet.
Some start off quite quickly. Others take it slow.
Some have tried this trail before and know just where to go.

The first stop is with Lady Luck. She's just a few hills in.
The babies there all laugh and play, making Lady grin.

She peek-a-boos and pat-a-cakes and spins them 'round and 'round.
She knows their parents won't be long and listens for their sound.

"Welcome! Meet your children!" she bellows down the line.

And so they do just as she says. The hikers hit their stride.
The second stretch goes on and on, weaving side to side.

Then suddenly ahead they see a sign for Father Time.
Up to his door are steps galore, and everyone must climb.

"Shh!" Time says as they approach. "Please don't make a peep!
I've rocked your babes, tucked them in, and sung them all to sleep."

He eyes the tired faces of the parents without cribs
and warmly says, "Don't worry! There's help beyond that ridge."

Off they go, back on the path, this bold and driven bunch—
until they hear a voice ahead: "Hey! Come inside for lunch!"

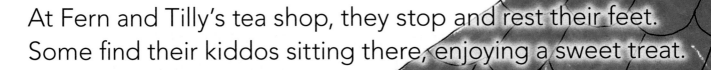

At Fern and Tilly's tea shop, they stop and rest their feet.
Some find their kiddos sitting there, enjoying a sweet treat.

"Join us, mums and dads! There's plenty for you too.
We've kept your babies' bellies full while waiting here for you."

The others turn to Tilly and wonder what to do.

"Come," she says kindly. "We've got options here for you."

"Try our clomid coffee and surrogate souffles, adopt-tarts, donor donuts, and frozen egg buffets."

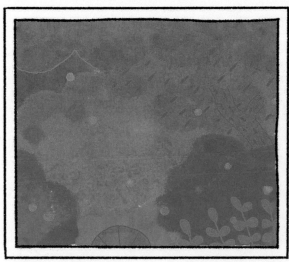

She also shows them maps of many other paths to try.

Some decide to trek towards the Bayou IUI.

At the Bayou IUI, there's so much to explore.
Each day there, the bayou babes are learning more and more.

So lush and dense the bayou is, the babes are hard to spot.
Some parents do four, five, six laps before they find their lot.

Others leave the bayou knowing that it's time
to head toward the Ivy Edge, the steepest of its kind.

The path is all-consuming, led by a guide named Wanda.
It's lined with prickly bushes, which nobody is fond of.

It's also lined with hope, with family and friends,
and strangers who have paved the way up to the Ivy Edge.

The moment comes, and someone cries,
"We made it! There they are!"
The babies by the Ivy Edge are shining, bright as stars.

Every day around the globe, babies crawl and climb.

Some have come from Lady Luck and some from Father Time.

Some of them just needed some of Fern and Tilly's tea,

while Bayou babes were off exploring all there is to see.

And some of them were shining up by the Ivy Edge.

But when they're all together, you can't tell which is which.

Printed in the United States
by Baker & Taylor Publisher Services